EARTH'S CYCLES IN ACTION

THE NITROGEN CYCLE

By Diane Dakers

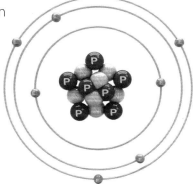

A nitrogen atom

E Electron

N Neutron

P Proton

CRABTREE
Publishing Company
www.crabtreebooks.com

Crabtree Publishing Company
www.crabtreebooks.com

Author: Diane Dakers
Publishing plan research and development:
Reagan Miller
Project coordinator: Mark Sachner,
Water Buffalo Books
Editors: Mark Sachner, Shirley Duke
Proofreader: Shannon Welbourn
Editorial director: Kathy Middleton
Photo researcher: Ruth Owen
Designer: Westgraphix/Tammy West
Contributing writer and indexer: Suzy Gazlay
Production coordinator and prepress technician:
Margaret Amy Salter
Print coordinator: Katherine Berti
Science, reading, and curriculum consultant:
Suzy Gazlay, M.A.; Recipient, Presidential Award
for Excellence in Science Teaching

Written, developed, and produced by
Water Buffalo Books

Photographs and reproductions:
Front Cover: Shutterstock: Dudarev Mikhail

Interior: Alamy: pp. 8, 16 (left), 36 (top).
Science Photo Library: pp. 15 (right), 19, 21, 40 (bottom), 41. **Shutterstock:** pp. 1, 3, 4, 5, 6, 7 (top), 9, 10, 11, 12, 13, 14, 15 (left), 16 (right), 16 (bottom), 17, 18, 20, 22, 23, 24, 25, 26, 27, 28, 29, 30, 31, 32, 33, 34, 35, 36 (bottom), 37, 38, 39, 40 (top), 42 (background, top, upper right), 43 (background, top, upper right, lower right, center left), 44–45, 46, 47, 48. **Superstock:** p. 7 (bottom). **Suzy Gazlay:** pp. 42 (lower left, lower right), 43 (top center, upper left, center left, lower left, center right).

Library and Archives Canada Cataloguing in Publication

Dakers, Diane, author
        The nitrogen cycle / Diane Dakers.

(Earth's cycles in action)
Includes index.
Issued in print and electronic formats.
ISBN 978-0-7787-0599-4 (bound).--ISBN 978-0-7787-0623-6 (pbk.).--
ISBN 978-1-4271-7626-4 (pdf).--ISBN 978-1-4271-7622-6 (html)

        1. Nitrogen cycle--Juvenile literature. I. Title.

QH344.D353 2014   j577'.145   C2014-903933-6
                                            C2014-903934-4

Library of Congress Cataloging-in-Publication Data

Dakers, Diane, author.
 The nitrogen cycle / Diane Dakers.
        pages cm. -- (Earth's cycles in action)
 Includes index.
 ISBN 978-0-7787-0599-4 (reinforced library binding) --
 ISBN 978-0-7787-0623-6 (pbk.) --
 ISBN 978-1-4271-7626-4 (electronic pdf) --
 ISBN 978-1-4271-7622-6 (electronic html)
 1. Nitrogen cycle--Juvenile literature. I. Title.

QH344.D38 2015
577.145--dc23
                                    2014032599

Crabtree Publishing Company
www.crabtreebooks.com   1-800-387-7650

Printed in Canada/102014/EF20140925

**Published
in Canada
Crabtree Publishing**
616 Welland Ave.
St. Catharines, Ontario
L2M 5V6

**Published in
the United States
Crabtree Publishing**
PMB 59051
350 Fifth Ave., 59th Floor
New York, NY 10118

**Published in the
United Kingdom
Crabtree Publishing**
Maritime House
Basin Road North, Hove
BN41 1WR

**Published
in Australia
Crabtree Publishing**
3 Charles Street
Coburg North
VIC, 3058

Contents

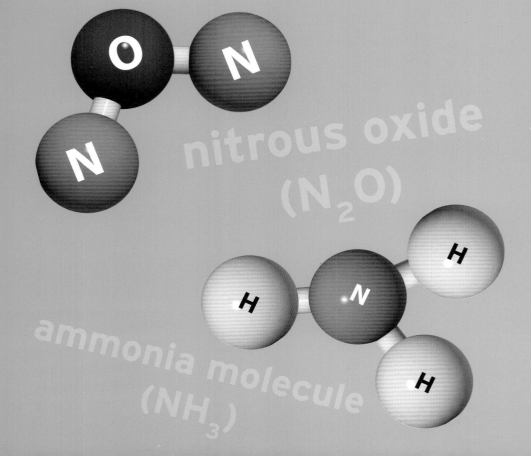

CHAPTER 1

Why Care About Nitrogen?

Every known living thing—plant and animal—contains nitrogen. About three percent of your body is nitrogen. That means, if you weigh 100 pounds (45 kilograms), you contain about three pounds (1.4 kg) of nitrogen. That's about how much a large guinea pig weighs!

Tiny Building Blocks

Everything in the world is made up of **atoms** and **molecules**. Atoms and molecules are submicroscopic. This means they are so small that they cannot be seen with an ordinary microscope. Atoms are individual building blocks, and molecules are combinations of those building blocks. The **Periodic Table of Elements** lists the 118 known types of atoms. For example, one of those atoms is nitrogen, represented on the periodic table as N.

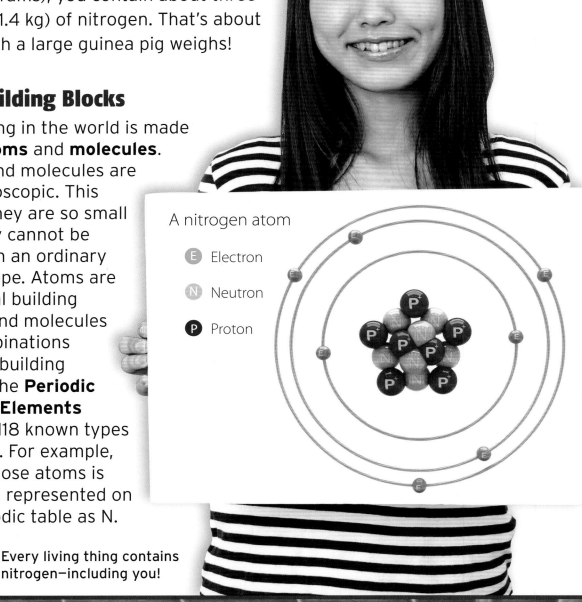

A nitrogen atom

- **E** Electron
- **N** Neutron
- **P** Proton

Every living thing contains nitrogen—including you!

Another is oxygen, represented by the letter O. When one nitrogen atom combines with two oxygen atoms, they form a molecule called NO_2. This is nitrogen dioxide, a brown gas that is sometimes seen hanging over big cities. In combination with other toxic gases, this brown haze is also called smog.

The atoms that combine to form the most important molecules in the human body are carbon (C), hydrogen (H), phosphorus (P), oxygen (O), and nitrogen (N).

In the center of each atom is a **nucleus**, which contains **protons** and **neutrons**. Surrounding the nucleus is a cloud of **electrons**. The number of electrons is the same as the number of protons in an atom. Nitrogen has seven protons and seven electrons.

Charting the Atoms

The Periodic Table of Elements shows all the chemical **elements** known to exist. Each element is made up of atoms of that type of element. For example, the element nitrogen consists of nitrogen atoms. Some elements occur naturally, and others are developed in laboratories and are therefore synthetic, or human-made. The periodic table lists them in order of increasing atomic number, or the number of protons in the atom's nucleus. Nitrogen is number 7 in the table.

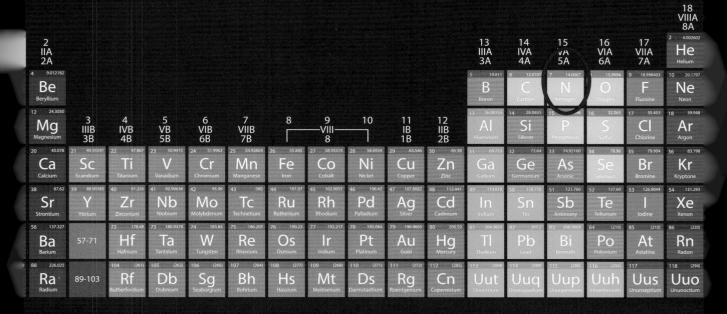

Periodic Table of Elements

Airborne Nitrogen

Nitrogen is one of about 90 elements, or pure substances, that exist naturally on Earth. The only place pure nitrogen is found is in the air that surrounds us. About 78 percent of our air is made up of nitrogen gas, or N_2. That means every breath you take is mostly made of pure nitrogen. (The rest is oxygen, with tiny bits of other gases mixed in.)

Pure nitrogen is a tasteless, colorless, and odorless gas. It is also called an **inert** gas. This means that it doesn't easily bond, or join, with other elements. Given the opportunity, a nitrogen atom will tend to bond only with another nitrogen atom. The two form such a strong connection that nitrogen gas (N_2) does not react easily with other atoms. That's not to say it doesn't react, or bond, with other atoms. It just means it takes a lot of energy for that to happen.

Because nitrogen gas is so **stable**, it is used in situations where chemical reactions might cause problems. Potato chip bags, for example, are filled with nitrogen gas. If the bags were filled with regular air, the oxygen in that air would make the chips become stale.

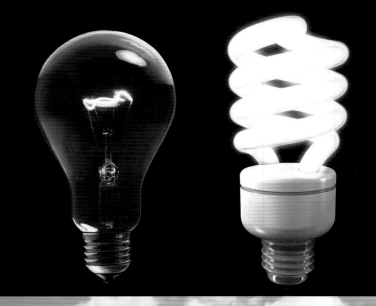

This ordinary light bulb (left) contains nitrogen gas, which doesn't catch fire when the metal **filament**, or wire, inside gets hot. In many parts of the world, these bulbs are being replaced by compact fluorescent lamps, or CFLs (right). CFLs require far less electricity and last a lot longer than ordinary bulbs. They can reduce costs, save energy, and help the environment by cutting down on the use of natural resources needed to produce electricity.

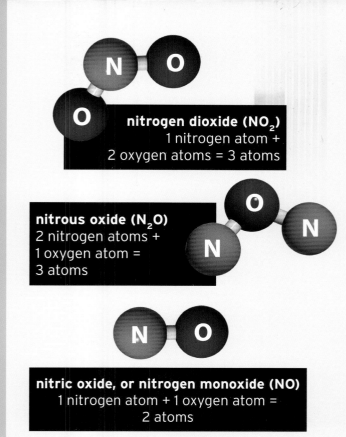

nitrogen dioxide (NO$_2$)
1 nitrogen atom +
2 oxygen atoms = 3 atoms

nitrous oxide (N$_2$O)
2 nitrogen atoms +
1 oxygen atom =
3 atoms

nitric oxide, or nitrogen monoxide (NO)
1 nitrogen atom + 1 oxygen atom =
2 atoms

MAKING SENSE OF CYCLES

There are many molecules made of nitrogen and oxygen. Many have the word "oxide" in their name, and as a group they are called nitrogen oxides. "Oxides" refers to the oxygen part of the molecule. Three common ones are nitrogen dioxide (NO$_2$), nitrous oxide (N$_2$O), and nitric oxide (NO), which is sometimes called nitrogen monoxide.

Here is one useful way to keep these **compounds** straight. As you read this book, keep a list of each of these three common nitrogen compounds. Also list as many ways that each occurs in nature or human activity as you can find.

If crash test dummies could talk, they would sing the praises of airbags inflated with nitrogen gas! Not only do the bags protect us from impact injuries, but the nitrogen is so stable that it reduces the chance of explosions and fire.

Some historical documents are preserved in airtight containers filled with nitrogen gas. The United States Declaration of Independence, for example, is stored in this way. If it were to come into contact with air, the oxygen in the air would eventually destroy the document.

One very important place nitrogen is used is in cars. Nitrogen gas is what inflates the airbags, and protects you, in a car when it crashes. Because nitrogen is so stable, it won't react with other elements and cause an explosion in case there's a fire.

Nitrogen Compounded

Nitrogen gas is one of the most abundant, or plentiful, elements around us. Because it doesn't easily bond with other atoms, not many nitrogen compounds exist naturally on Earth. Some other types of atoms do link up with nitrogen, however, and form compounds.

Protein molecules in animals and plants contain nitrogen. Protein is part of our cells, organs, bones, and more. We can't survive without it, and therefore we can't survive without nitrogen! A few nitrogen compounds exist in soil and water. A small amount of a compound called nitrous oxide gas (N_2O) exists naturally in our atmosphere. A compound called sodium nitrate ($NaNO_3$), or Chile saltpeter, is found underground in South America. This white crystal is used in the manufacturing of fertilizers, gunpowder, and explosives.

A nurse treating a wart with liquid nitrogen.

Liquid Nitrogen

In its natural state on Earth, nitrogen is a gas. But you may have heard of liquid nitrogen. This is a form of pure nitrogen that has been cooled to such a low temperature that it has become, as its name states, a liquid.

Because liquid nitrogen is so cold, it is used to fast-freeze some foods for transportation and storage. For example, if you dip raspberries in liquid nitrogen, the berries will freeze instantly, making it easier to package and ship them.

Liquid nitrogen is used in hospitals and labs to preserve blood and tissue samples until they are needed. It is also used to remove skin growths or irregularities such as warts, birthmarks, and skin cancers. Liquid nitrogen fast-freezes the skin it contacts. This destroys the unwanted tissue so it can be removed.

Other than these few substances, most nitrogen compounds are synthetic, or human-made. Some are used to make colorful dyes for fabrics. Some are used in fireworks and explosives. TNT, which is short for *trinitrotoluene*, is an explosive mostly used for military purposes. Dynamite is another explosive made from nitrogen compounds. It is often used in mines and to demolish buildings. In *Looney Tunes* cartoons Wile E. Coyote uses both when he tries to blow up the Roadrunner!

One particularly common nitrogen compound is called **ammonia**. It is used to make fertilizers that help farmers grow healthy crops. This same compound is also produced naturally in soil. And this is where the nitrogen cycle, which moves this essential element everywhere it is needed, comes in!

An apartment building during a controlled blast. Triggered by carefully placed dynamite, made from nitrogen compounds, the blast was designed to cause the building to implode, or collapse, inward.

CHAPTER 2

Cycles Make the World Go 'Round

A gardener plants a sunflower seed. Before long, the seed sprouts and grows into a sunflower. The sunflower produces seeds, which fall to the ground. Eventually, those seeds sprout and grow into new sunflowers, which produce more seeds. These new seeds then fall to the ground, sprout, and grow more sunflowers, which produce more seeds ... and so on. This is an example of a cycle, a pattern of related processes or events that happen over and over again. Like a circle, a cycle has no beginning and ending. It just keeps going and going and going...

Sunflowers in full bloom

Dried head of sunflower, showing seeds

Fresh sunflower seeds

Sunflower seedling

Green sunflower plant

The life cycle of a sunflower plant

Cycles of Life

Our planet is filled with many cycles. In fact, every day is a cycle, and so is every year.

As Earth rotates, or spins, the cycle of day and night occurs. In the night sky, another cycle occurs as the Moon orbits Earth.

Earth's orbit around the Sun creates the changing of the seasons.

Spring, summer, fall, winter: that's a cycle that happens over and over again, year after year.

Some of Earth's natural cycles are less easy to notice, and many happen without us even knowing about them. Some occur at such a **microscopic** level that we can't see them. One such cycle is the nitrogen cycle. We can't see it happening, but we can't live without it.

In this artist's rendition of Earth in space, several cycles are evident: the cycle of day and night; the Moon in the night sky orbiting Earth and reflecting sunlight as it joins our planet's orbit around the Sun; and clouds in Earth's **atmosphere** that have been part of the cycle bringing fresh water to the planet for billions of years.

The Nitrogen Cycle

As a natural element that cannot be created or destroyed, all the nitrogen that exists on the planet is recycled. This means that it is used over and over again in a variety of forms.

Every known animal and plant needs some form of nitrogen to stay alive.

Every living thing is also part of the nitrogen cycle that moves this essential element throughout Earth. Nitrogen travels from the air to soil to plants to animals, and back to the soil and the air. The nitrogen cycle also happens in bodies of water.

For millions of years, the nitrogen cycle has gone on in perfect balance. In the last one hundred years or so, however, the cycle has started losing its balance. Human activities have been upsetting the cycle's natural harmony, and that could lead to all kinds of problems for life on Earth.

Nitrogen is available to sustain life in the air, in the soil, and in the water. Today, humans share, with nature, the responsibility of keeping that cycle in balance.

Nitrogen Facts

- The chemical symbol for nitrogen is N.
- Nitrogen was discovered in 1772 by two different scientists—Scottish chemist Daniel Rutherford, and Swedish chemist Carl Scheele.
- When it was first discovered, nitrogen was called "**noxious** air," "burnt air," and "foul air," because animals could not breathe it.
- French chemist Jean-Antoine Chaptal named it "nitrogen" in 1790.
- Nitrogen is the seventh most common element in the universe—after hydrogen, helium, oxygen, carbon, neon, and iron.
- It is the fourth most common element in the human body, after oxygen, carbon, and hydrogen.
- All the nitrogen in the universe comes from explosions inside stars.

All of Earth's life forms, including the plant, ladybug, and butterfly shown here, play a role in keeping the nitrogen cycle in order. They also benefit from the exchange of nitrogen between the air, soil, and even the morning dew on this blade of grass.

Understanding the importance of nitrogen and a balanced nitrogen cycle will help us keep our planet and ourselves healthy. Because the nitrogen cycle is a *cycle*, it doesn't have a beginning or an end point. But we have to start somewhere, so let's start by looking at what happens to nitrogen in soil!

CHAPTER 3

The Nitrogen Cycle in the Earth

All plants and animals need nitrogen to survive, and the air is full of nitrogen gas. Take a deep breath in. You've just inhaled a lot of nitrogen. Now breathe out. You've just exhaled all the nitrogen you breathed in. Your body didn't use any of it. Plants and animals can't use the nitrogen in the air. So how do we, and other living things, get nitrogen in a form we can use? First of all, the nitrogen has to go underground.

The Underground World of Nitrogen

Many types of **bacteria** live in the soil. Bacteria are single-celled organisms, or life forms, so small that you need a microscope to see them. Some bacteria in the soil take nitrogen gas from the air and change it into compounds that help plants grow. These bacteria, and some bacteria in water, are the only organisms that can use nitrogen gas directly from the air. Without these bacteria, no living thing would get the nitrogen it needs to exist.

Different bacteria are responsible for different steps in the nitrogen cycle. One step in the cycle is called **nitrogen fixation**. In this step, certain types of bacteria absorb nitrogen gas (N_2) from the air. In the process, the two nitrogen atoms are separated. Some of the nitrogen

This handful of dirt is loaded with nitrogen compounds that all life forms need to live and grow. These compounds are created out of nitrogen gas that is absorbed into the ground during the nitrogen cycle.

Bacteria are extremely small living things that are found everywhere on Earth. These single-cell organisms are so tiny, it would take a million of them to cover a pinhead!

Bacteria live in the soil, in your food, in animals, in plants, in the air, even in your body. They have been found everywhere from near-boiling hot springs to frozen Antarctic ice.

Bacteria have a bad reputation. That's because some of them can make us sick. Most are helpful, though. There are hundreds of thousands of species, or types, of bacteria on Earth. Scientists say that 99 percent of them, such as the ones involved in the nitrogen cycle, are **beneficial**, or valuable.

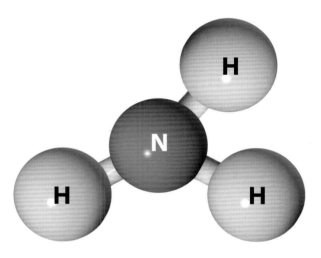

1 nitrogen atom +
3 hydrogen atoms =
1 ammonia molecule
(NH_3)

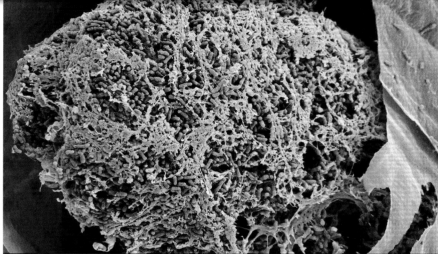

This color-enhanced photo, taken by an electron microscope, shows soil bacteria (green) living on the root of a bean plant. The bacteria fix, or convert, nitrogen from the air into ammonia, which benefits the plant. The plant in turn produces compounds that provide energy to the bacteria. This symbiotic relationship helps both the plant and the bacteria.

combines with other atoms and is converted into compounds that bacteria use for food. Some of it is converted into a chemical called ammonia. Ammonia is a molecule made of one nitrogen atom and three hydrogen atoms. Its chemical formula is NH_3.

In some cases, these bacteria which are called nitrogen-fixing bacteria, actually live inside a plant. They live in **nodules**, or bulges, on a plant's roots. These bacteria have a **symbiotic relationship** with the plants they inhabit. This means that the plant and the bacteria each get something positive out of the arrangement. The bacteria get an ideal place to live, and the plant gets a built-in source of nitrogen in the form of ammonia. This symbiotic relationship with bacteria happens in a family of plants called **legumes**. Legumes include such plants as peas, beans, peanuts, and clover.

Most plants can't get their nitrogen needs met with ammonia, however, and more nitrogen-fixing bacteria live in the soil than in the roots. At this point, then, other bacteria become part of the process. These bacteria—the ones that live outside of plants—create a new nitrogen compound. This step in the nitrogen cycle is called **nitrification**.

Broad beans

Nitrogen-fixing nodules on the roots of a broad bean plant

Broad bean plants

During nitrification, different types of bacteria take the ammonia from the soil and combine it with oxygen. This process creates molecules called nitrates. Plants then draw these nitrates into their roots. The plants are able to use these nitrates to make proteins and other substances they need to grow and thrive.

More News About Nitrogen

While some bacteria in the soil convert nitrogen gas in the air into a form of nitrogen that plants can use, other types of bacteria do the opposite. They convert extra nitrogen in the soil into nitrogen gas that is returned to the air.

This step in the nitrogen cycle is called **denitrification**.

Denitrification by bacteria isn't the only way that Earth returns nitrogen to the atmosphere. When volcanoes erupt, one of the gases they spew into the air is nitrogen gas.

The combination of all these bacterial and volcanic processes, along with lightning, keeps the amounts of nitrogen in our air and in our soil in perfect balance. Unfortunately, human activities can upset this natural balance.

This diagram illustrates three important steps in the nitrogen cycle: nitrogen fixation, nitrification, and denitrification.

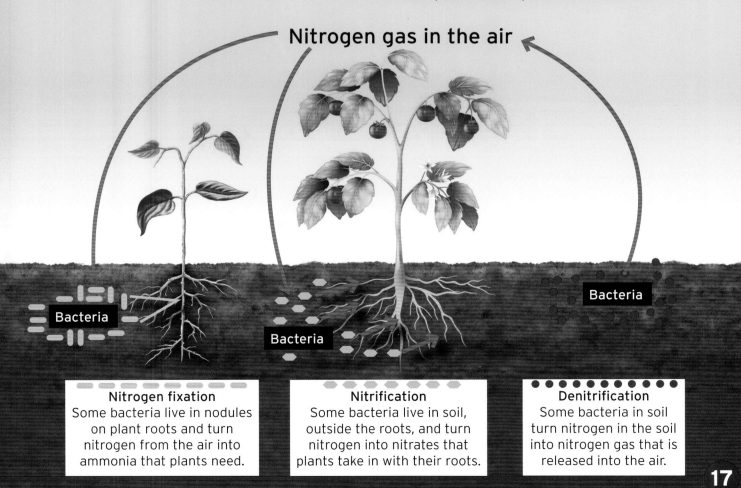

Nitrogen gas in the air

Bacteria

Bacteria

Bacteria

Nitrogen fixation
Some bacteria live in nodules on plant roots and turn nitrogen from the air into ammonia that plants need.

Nitrification
Some bacteria live in soil, outside the roots, and turn nitrogen into nitrates that plants take in with their roots.

Denitrification
Some bacteria in soil turn nitrogen in the soil into nitrogen gas that is released into the air.

Every time lightning flashes across the sky, it changes some nitrogen gas in the air into a nitrogen compound that plants can use.

Lightning has so much energy that it splits apart the molecules of nitrogen gas (N_2) in the air. During a lightning storm, these nitrogen atoms react with the water molecules in rain to form ammonia. The ammonia then binds with oxygen atoms in the air to make compounds called nitrates. The falling rain carries these new compounds to the ground.

The lightning "fixes" the nitrogen into forms that plants can use in this way. The process is similar to how nitrogen-fixing bacteria convert nitrogen in the soil. Lightning produces about 10 percent of Earth's fixed nitrogen.

It's Raining Nitrogen

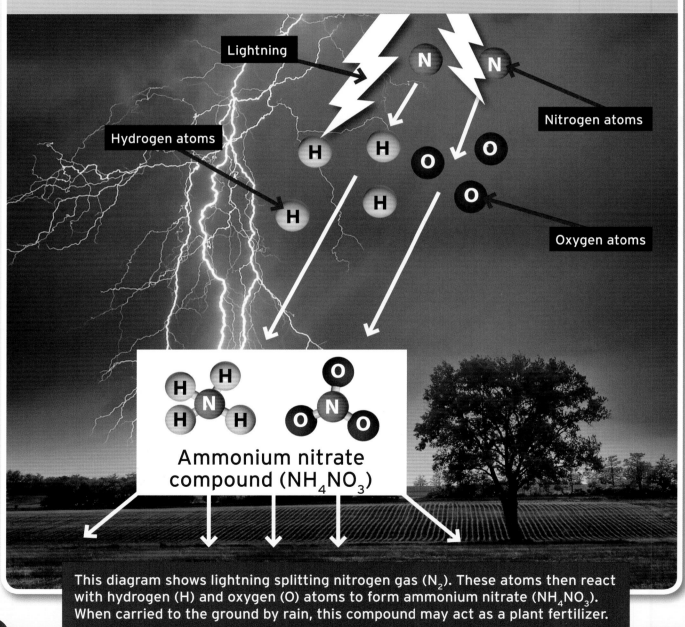

Lightning

Nitrogen atoms

Hydrogen atoms

Oxygen atoms

Ammonium nitrate compound (NH_4NO_3)

This diagram shows lightning splitting nitrogen gas (N_2). These atoms then react with hydrogen (H) and oxygen (O) atoms to form ammonium nitrate (NH_4NO_3). When carried to the ground by rain, this compound may act as a plant fertilizer.

On land, bacteria in the soil take nitrogen from the air and convert it into molecules that plants need. The same process happens in rivers, lakes, and oceans. It's just a different kind of bacteria that make this conversion in water.

The **aquatic** type of bacteria in this part of the nitrogen cycle are called **cyanobacteria**, or **blue-green algae**. In spite of their name, blue-green algae are actually blue-green bacteria that live in the water.

Like soil-based bacteria, blue-green algae absorb nitrogen gas from the air, then "fix" the nitrogen. That means they convert it to ammonia, which they release into the water. Oxygen in the water combines with ammonia to form nitrates. There are also some bacteria that do the same thing. Aquatic plants absorb this usable form of nitrogen from the water.

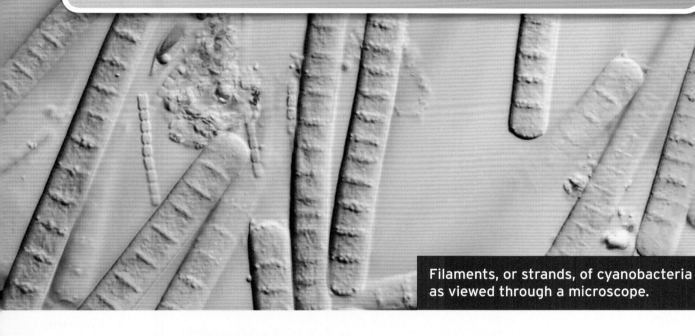

Filaments, or strands, of cyanobacteria as viewed through a microscope.

As we burn fuels like gasoline and coal, some harmful nitrogen compounds are released into the atmosphere. As farmers and gardeners add more and more nitrogen-rich fertilizers to the soil, the balance of nitrogen in that soil changes. Excess nitrogen can wash into our waterways and contaminate aquatic ecosystems.

By understanding the nitrogen cycle, we can do our part to help restore the balance of nitrogen on the planet. We already know that tiny bacteria in the soil and water convert nitrogen to a form that plants can use. So what do plants do with all that nitrogen? Well, that takes us to the next step in the nitrogen cycle.

CHAPTER 4

The Nitrogen Cycle in Plants

On a nice day, you might take a walk through a field, meadow, or forest. On your walk, you'll probably see grasses, flowers, and trees swaying gently in the breeze. Those plants may look as if they're doing nothing but soaking up sunshine in the fresh air. In fact, though, there's a lot going on inside those plants. You just can't see the activity, because it happens on such a small scale. One important process going on in them is the plants' portion of the nitrogen cycle.

Nitrogen Factory

All plants need nitrogen. They use it to produce seeds, flowers, and fruits. It helps them grow and become full-bodied and strong. First of all, though, they have to absorb the nitrogen.

Even though air is mostly made of nitrogen gas, plants can't use that form of nitrogen. Instead, they take their nitrogen from the soil.

Bacteria in the soil transform nitrogen in the air into forms of nitrogen that plants can use—ammonia and nitrates. Plants absorb these compounds through their roots. Then they use the nitrogen to build other compounds they need to live, grow, and stay healthy. This step in the nitrogen cycle is called nitrogen **assimilation**.

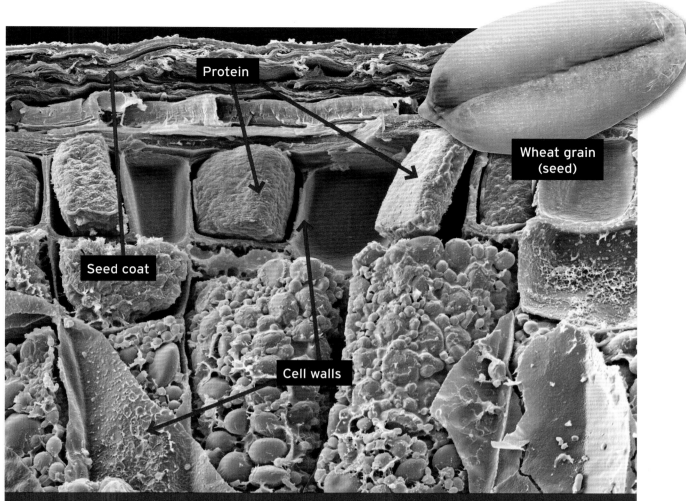

Protein

Wheat grain (seed)

Seed coat

Cell walls

Upper right inset: a grain (or seed) of wheat. In the larger photo, taken by an electron microscope, a section of a similar seed shows many of the substances that make up the seed. Included among them are molecules of the nitrogen compound protein, shown in green, and cell walls. Cell walls are a layer that exists around certain kinds of cells in plants and plant-like species. They are not part of the cell itself, but they support and protect the cell. Some cell walls also help organisms maintain their shape.

Some of the most important nitrogen compounds created inside plants are **amino acids** and proteins.

Amino acids are molecules made of four different types of atoms—nitrogen, carbon, oxygen, and hydrogen. Different combinations of these atoms form different kinds of amino acids.

Chains of amino acids form proteins. The chains might consist of just two amino acids, or they could be made of thousands of amino acids linked together! The number and type of amino acids in the chain determine what job a protein does, what role it plays in the plant's life.

Like humans and other animals, plants need protein to grow and

One of the most important things a plant does with nitrogen is use it to produce **chlorophyll**. That's the chemical in the leaves that makes a plant green. It's also a key ingredient in **photosynthesis**, the process that green plants use to make their food.

For photosynthesis to happen, a plant needs three ingredients. One is water. A plant's roots absorb water from the soil. The water travels up the stem and to the leaves. At the same time the leaves are drawing water from within the plant, they are also collecting another key ingredient, carbon dioxide gas, from the air around the plant. Meanwhile, chlorophyll in the leaves is absorbing sunlight. With sunlight, the list of ingredients required for photosynthesis is complete.

Through chemical reactions in the plant's leaves, photosynthesis breaks down carbon dioxide and water and releases two new compounds. One is a type of sugar, which feeds the plant. The other is oxygen, which is released into the air. That oxygen keeps humans and other animals alive!

stay healthy. Some proteins help plant cells keep their structure, or shape. Others help plants fight off diseases.

One kind of protein, called **enzymes**, drives all the functions and chemical reactions that happen inside plants. For example, enzymes drive plant growth, seed production, and photosynthesis. Photosynthesis is the process that green plants use to convert water, sunlight, and carbon dioxide gas into food.

Sunlight

Oxygen

Carbon dioxide

Water

Sunlight, carbon dioxide, and water: the three main ingredients a green plant needs to produce its own food through photosynthesis. In the process, the plant also releases oxygen into the air.

Plants get their nitrates from soil, but there are many nitrates out in the world that don't come from such a natural source.

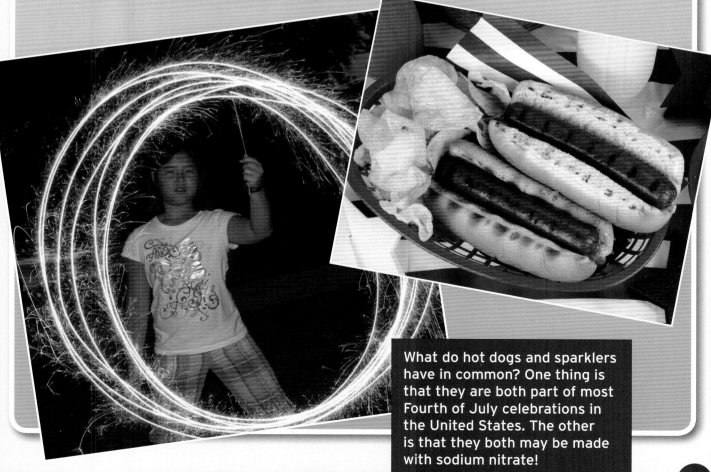

The Great Nitrate

One thing all nitrates have in common is that they contain one nitrogen atom and three oxygen atoms. Nitrates combine with many other elements to make new chemicals with many different purposes. Most of these compounds are synthetic, or human-made.

Sodium nitrate, for example, is a common food preservative used in meats such as hot dogs, bacon, and beef jerky. Even though sodium nitrate *is* found in nature, most of it is made in laboratories. Also called Chile saltpeter, sodium nitrate is used in fertilizers, firecrackers, and gunpowder. So is potassium nitrate—whose common name is saltpeter (without the "Chile"). Potassium nitrate is a common ingredient in toothpastes and mouthwashes designed for people with sensitive teeth.

Aluminum nitrate is used in antiperspirants, which are found in most brands of underarm deodorant. Zinc nitrate is used in dyes. Calcium nitrate is used to help concrete set quickly. Silver nitrate is used in photographic film. These are just a few of the common nitrates and their uses.

What do hot dogs and sparklers have in common? One thing is that they are both part of most Fourth of July celebrations in the United States. The other is that they both may be made with sodium nitrate!

The Next Steps for Nitrogen

When plants die, they begin to decay, or rot. When that happens, dead plant material returns to the soil and takes all its nitrogen with it. That's when another step in the nitrogen cycle takes place.

Remember those bacteria in the soil that convert nitrogen gas to compounds that plants can use? Well, in this step, *different* bacteria in the soil break down the nitrogen compounds in rotting plants. They convert the nitrogen to ammonia and release it back into the soil. This step in the nitrogen cycle is called **ammonification**.

Once the ammonia is in the soil, another type of bacteria converts it to nitrates that plants can use.

And yet another type of bacteria converts ammonia into nitrogen gas, which returns to the air. In these ways, the nitrogen cycle continues.

Not all plants are simply left to rot in the soil, though. Often, animals come along and eat plants. That means they also eat the nitrogen contained in plants. And when animals become involved, they lead the nitrogen cycle in another direction.

Rotten apples

Just like plants on land, plants in water need nitrogen to make amino acids, proteins, and other nitrogen compounds.

In the water, certain bacteria "fix" the nitrogen into ammonia and others convert ammonia to nitrates. Oxygen in the water also converts ammonia to nitrates. This is a form of nitrogen that aquatic plants, just like land plants, can use.

When water plants die and sink to the bottom of a body of water, they also release ammonia. Bacteria deep in the water and on the sea floor transform the ammonia into nitrates and nitrogen gas. These are released into the water, and the nitrogen cycle continues.

Aquatic Plants Need Nitrogen, Too!

Nitrogen gas in the air

Aquatic plants die, and bacteria convert the nitrogen in this dead plant material into nitrates and nitrogen gas.

Bacteria in water convert nitrogen into ammonia and nitrates that aquatic plants can use.

CHAPTER 5

The Nitrogen Cycle in Animals

All animals, including humans, need nitrogen. That means all animals need plants, because plants are full of nitrogen compounds. Plants contain nitrogen in the form of proteins, nitrates, and amino acids. Eating plants, or eating organisms that eat plants, supplies animals with all the nitrogen they need to grow, build muscles and organs, and stay healthy.

Skin, antlers, beaks: Almost every body part of every animal needs proteins to work properly.

Building the Building Blocks

Without nitrogen, there would be no proteins. Without proteins, animals could not exist. Almost every body part of every animal contains some kind of protein. For example, blood, skin, brains, eyes, nerves, beaks, antlers—all these and more contain protein. Proteins like enzymes drive chemical reactions that keep body parts running properly. Other proteins help keep us and other animals from getting sick.

Proteins are made up of chains of smaller molecules called amino acids. We already know that these molecules contain four different types of atoms—nitrogen, oxygen, carbon, and hydrogen. These key ingredients create hundreds of different amino acids on Earth. But most proteins in most organisms are made of the same 20 amino acids. As a group, these are called "standard amino acids." These are combined in different

Scientists estimate that the human body contains about 100,000 different kinds of protein. All these proteins are made of different combinations of just 20 amino acids joined in chains.

Amino acids are divided into two categories. "Essential" amino acids are the ones your body can't make on its own. That means you need to get them from your food. There are nine of those. The other 11 amino acids are called "non-essential." That doesn't mean they're not important! It just means that your body can make them, so you don't need to worry about including them in your diet.

ways in different numbers. The combinations make all kinds of different proteins with a variety of functions.

Nitrogen is also an important part of a protein called deoxyribonucleic acid. That's a mouthful! So we shorten the name and call it DNA. Every living thing, from the smallest bacteria to the largest blue whale, contains DNA.

DNA is a long, spiral-shaped molecule that serves as a sort of instruction manual for every living thing—and every living thing has different DNA molecules. Even animals or plants in the same species, or group, have slightly different DNA. That means that no two people, or snails, or maple trees, or sunflowers, are *exactly* the same. Sometimes two flowers, for example, might *look* identical. Within their cells, however, where their DNA lies, they have slight differences. Those differences may be smaller than even an ordinary microscope can detect, but they are there.

Our DNA makes all of us different, even in ways that we cannot see!

A Body's Blueprint

DNA is a complicated set of molecules found in the cells of every living thing. It's like computer code that tells a body or plant how to grow, how to move, how to live, and what to look like.

Human bodies have more than 200 different kinds of cells, and each has a different job to do. The DNA tells each cell what its job is. It might be a blood cell, a bone cell, or a muscle cell.

As the computer model shown here illustrates, DNA is made of long strings of building blocks called nucleotides. There are only four different nucleotides, but one DNA strand can be made up of hundreds of thousands of nucleotides!

Imagine you have 1,000 beads in four different colors. Those beads represent the four kinds of nucleotides. Now imagine all the different ways you could string those colored beads together into a necklace. A DNA molecule is like that colored string of beads, only there are hundreds of times more "beads," or nucleotides, in a DNA chain. That means there are millions of different possible ways those four nucleotides could be combined into DNA chains.

The DNA of every human being on the planet is 99.9 percent the same as that of every other human being. That last 0.1 percent is what makes us all so different. What's even more interesting is that the DNA of humans and chimpanzees is 98 percent the same—and humans and cabbages have about half their DNA in common. Believe it or not!

DNA carries all the information about what a particular organism will look like. What color will this animal be? How tall will this plant grow? When that baby grows up, will her eyes be light or dark brown? It also tells amino acids within an organism how to create the proteins it needs to survive. DNA is like a computer program that tells a life form everything it needs to know about how to live, how to look, how to grow, how to reproduce. Everything.

From N to Pee

When a body is finished with its nitrogen, or if it has extra nitrogen, it has to get rid of it. Otherwise, excess nitrogen would build up and become toxic, causing diseases that can harm or even kill the organism.

To begin the process of the **elimination**, or removal, of nitrogen, proteins in the body break down to form simpler nitrogen compounds. Different animals get rid of these compounds in different ways.

In aquatic animals, such as fish, lobsters, and starfish, the proteins break down and form ammonia. These creatures pass the ammonia—and therefore, nitrogen—through their gills, skin, or pores, into the water.

Animals that lay eggs on land, including birds, reptiles, and insects, release a different form of nitrogen. It's called uric acid, and it becomes a globby sort of sludge inside the animal. When the animal poops it out, it looks like, well, poop.

As for humans and other mammals, we pee out most of our excess nitrogen. Mammals also excrete, or release, some excess nitrogen in their solid wastes, or feces (poop), but our main way of getting rid of excess nitrogen is through urine (pee). First, the nitrogen is converted to something called urea, which dissolves in the water in our bodies. When we urinate, the urea—and therefore, nitrogen—leaves our bodies in that stream of yellow called urine.

When excess nitrogen leaves our bodies through our waste matter (urine and feces), it enters the sewage system along with other waste water. Sadly, not all the sewage that we create is treated and purified so it can return to the environment as clean water. Much of it, like that shown here, is dumped with other pollutants directly into our oceans, lakes, and rivers.

Key to the Nitrogen Cycle

The nitrogen cycle consists of five main steps:

1. **Fixation**
   Bacteria in soil and water turn atmospheric nitrogen (nitrogen in the air) into ammonia that plants need.

2. **Nitrification**
   Bacteria in soil and water turn ammonia into nitrates.

3. **Assimilation**
   Plants turn ammonia and nitrates into compounds they need to live and grow.

4. **Ammonification**
   Bacteria break down dead plants, animal waste, and animal bodies and convert nitrogen from this material into ammonia that is returned to the soil.

5. **Denitrification**
   Bacteria in soil turn nitrogen in the soil into nitrogen gas that is released into the air.

Assimilation

Atmospheric nitrogen (in the air)

Nitrogen fixation and nitrification

Denitrification

Assimilation

In the nitrogen cycle, nitrogen travels from the air to soil and water, to plants, to animals, and back to the soil, water, and air.

All the waste nitrogen from all these animals eventually finds its way into the world's waterways and soil and returns to the nitrogen cycle.

As we know, there are other ways that organisms return nitrogen to the nitrogen cycle. When a plant or animal dies, another animal might eat parts of it, but some parts are left on the ground to rot. When that happens, bacteria in the soil break down the nitrogen compounds in the dead plant or animal tissues. They convert the nitrogen to ammonia and release it into the soil.

This takes us to ammonification, the step in the nitrogen cycle that creates ammonia. Once the nitrogen is in the soil, other bacteria convert that nitrogen to compounds that plants can use. And the nitrogen cycle continues.

MAKING SENSE OF CYCLES

In the next chapter, you will read about various nitrogen compounds that can be harmful when they occur in large amounts in the air. Before you begin, make a list of some of the things you believe people in your community are doing that put harmful compounds into the air. As you read, compare your thoughts with the information in the text. How can this situation be changed? What can you do to help bring about these changes?

Atmospheric nitrogen (in the air)

Denitrification

Ammonification

CHAPTER 6

Messing with the N-Cycle

For millions of years, the nitrogen cycle has remained in perfect balance. It creates just the right mix of nitrogen compounds in the planet's air, soil, and water. As nitrogen moves through the cycle, it creates compounds that give life and energy to plants and animals. It reacts with other elements to form just the right mix of oxygen and nitrogen in the atmosphere. Nitrogen is also important to the process of converting plant and animal waste materials into useable compounds. In the last one hundred years, though, human activities have begun to disturb this perfectly balanced cycle.

Fertilizer: Too Much of a Good Thing?

An important part of the nitrogen cycle happens in the soil. Bacteria in the soil convert nitrogen in the air into ammonia and nitrates. These are compounds that plants need to grow.

When plants die, their rotting remains return nitrogen to the soil.

Plants harvested for food are not left to die in a field. That means they're not there to put nitrogen back into the soil. Eventually, all the nitrogen in the soil gets used up and it's no longer good for growing crops. When this happens, many farmers and gardeners add fertilizers to the soil. Most fertilizers contain natural substances, such as manure (animal wastes).

Harvesting machines like this combine are so efficient that they leave very little plant matter on the ground. Only the scraps of stems and leaves are left, and they do very little to replace the nitrogen and other nutrients that have been removed with the crops.

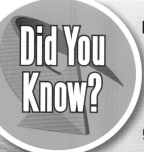

Did You Know?

In 1909, scientists discovered a way to make ammonia from nitrogen gas in the air. That made it possible to produce synthetic, or artificial, fertilizer. Since the middle of the 20th century, use of these synthetic fertilizers has skyrocketed. And with increased use of fertilizers, the level of excess nitrogen in the world's soil and waterways has also gone way up.

An overhead view of a crop duster spraying chemicals on a field in Idaho. Fertilizers help replace essential nitrogen in the soil. But they also contribute *excess* nitrogen that is washed by rainfall into waterways, where it may endanger aquatic wildlife.

They may also contain synthetic ammonia, nitrates, and other chemicals made by humans.

Fertilizers help build up the supply of nitrogen in soil, so plants will grow well again. The problem is that people have been using so much fertilizer that, in some places, there is too much nitrogen in the soil. This throws the nitrogen cycle out of balance. Overuse of fertilizers is the number one human activity disrupting the nitrogen cycle.

Eventually, rain washes excess fertilizers—and, therefore, nitrogen—into streams, rivers, lakes, and oceans. This added nitrogen helps some aquatic plants grow healthy and strong.

Unfortunately, it's not such a good thing for other plants and animals that live in that same body of water.

Blooming Algae

One group of aquatic organisms that thrive on excess nitrogen in the water are algae. Algae, although not plants, are plant-like life forms that can be as small as a single cell or as large as giant seaweed. Algae can be green, red, or yellowish-brown.

When nitrogen washes into rivers, lakes, and oceans, algae flourish. When this happens, the tiniest algae cause the biggest problems. They grow so fast that they form a sort of colored carpet across the top of the water. This is called an algal bloom.

The algal bloom blocks sunlight from other plants in the water. Algae don't live long. When they die, they rot and take oxygen out of the water. Without oxygen, plants and animals in the water can die. Algal blooms can also be toxic to people who accidentally drink the water around the blooms.

An algal bloom has made this tropical sea, which is normally blue, a bright green.

All that nitrogen makes certain aquatic plants grow so quickly and thickly that they block sunlight from other plants. Without sunlight, photosynthesis can't happen. Photosynthesis is how plants create food for themselves, and they can't survive without it. And without photosynthesis occurring, the amount of oxygen available to animals will be reduced.

When these excess plants die, they rot. The process of rotting uses up even more oxygen from the water. Fish and other aquatic wildlife can actually **suffocate** because they can't get enough oxygen.

It's not just farmers who sometimes use too much nitrogen-based fertilizer. Gardeners who grow plants in their backyards also use fertilizers. When they over-water their gardens or when it rains, water soaks into the ground. If they have used too much fertilizer, that water will become full of nitrogen compounds.

This nitrogen-filled water ends up in the storm drain system, which leads directly to local lakes and rivers. Excess nitrogen can lead to the overgrowth of certain aquatic life forms. These invasive species block sunlight and use up oxygen, endangering other life forms, plant and animal alike, in those bodies of water.

Backyard Nitrogen

This sign warns against dumping garbage or waste directly into a sewage system through storm drains.

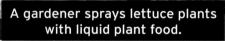

A gardener sprays lettuce plants with liquid plant food.

Unhealthy Air

Nitrogen gas (N_2) may be the main natural ingredient in our air, but other harmful nitrogen compounds are also out there. Human activity is increasing the amount of these unhealthy gases in our atmosphere.

People depend on **fossil fuels**, such as coal, oil, and natural gas. We use them to power cars, planes, boats, and other types of transportation. We use them to operate machinery, and to heat factories and homes.

When they burn, these fuels release harmful gases into our air, including nitric oxide (NO) and nitrogen dioxide (NO_2). Together, these and other compounds in the atmosphere are called nitrogen oxides.

The more fossil fuels we burn, the more nitrogen oxides go into our atmosphere. These gases cause problems for our Earth.

When it rains, nitrogen oxides mix with the water in the air and form nitric acid. The rainfall resulting from this combination produces **acid rain**. Acid rain can kill plants. It can also make lakes and rivers too acidic for certain marine creatures. Fish, snails, clams, and other aquatic animals may die if their habitat becomes too acidic.

Acid rain also dissolves certain kinds of stone, including limestone and marble. That means it can destroy buildings, outdoor sculptures, and gravestones made of these materials.

Nitrogen oxides in the air cause another problem—air pollution, or smog. When you see a brown haze hanging over a city on a hot day, what you are seeing is nitrogen dioxide (NO_2). Nitrogen dioxide is brown, and in addition to having a smell that is described as sharp and biting, it can create a burning sensation in your nose and airways. Nitric oxide (NO) is also present in smog. You just can't see it because it is a colorless gas. Both gases are harmful to humans if we breathe too much of them.

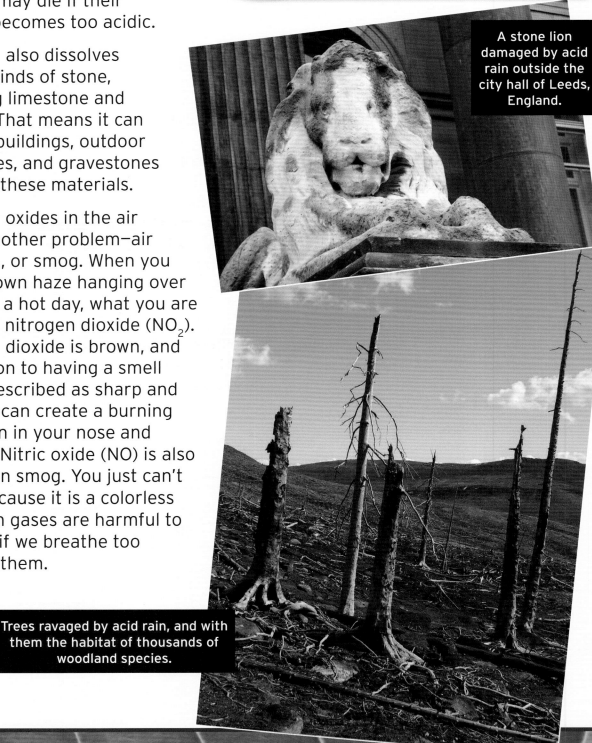

Did You Know?

Nitrogen oxides are not the only chemicals that cause acid rain. Sulfuric acid, made from sulfur in the air, and an oxygen compound called ozone also form acid rain.

A stone lion damaged by acid rain outside the city hall of Leeds, England.

Trees ravaged by acid rain, and with them the habitat of thousands of woodland species.

Guaranteed Analysis

Total Nitrogen (N) 5.0%
   0.4% Ammoniacal Nitrogen
   1.6% Other Water Soluble Nitrogen
   3.0% Water Insoluble Nitrogen*
Available Phosphate (P2O5) 3.0%
Soluble Potash (K2O) 3.0%
Calcium (Ca) 3.0%
Magnesium (Mg) 1.0%
   0.6% Water Soluble Magnesium (Mg)
Sulfur (S) 1.0%

Derived from: Hydrolyzed Feather Meal, Pasteurized Poultry Manure, Cocoa Meal, Bone Meal, Alfalfa Meal, Greensand, Humates, Sulfate of Potash, and Sulfate of Potash Magnesia.

   *Contains 3.0% Slow Release Nitrogen from Hydrolyzed Feather Meal, Pasteurized Poultry Manure, Cocoa Meal, Bone Meal, and Alfalfa Meal.

Guaranteed Analysis

Total Nitrogen 26%
   3.2% Ammoniacal Nitrogen
   9.7% Water Insoluble Nitrogen*
   3.4% Urea Nitrogen
   9.7% Other Water Soluble Nitrogen*
Available Phosphate (P2O5) 4%
Soluble Potash (K2O) 12%
Total Sulfur (S) 1.5%
   1.5% Combined Sulfur (S)

Nutrient Sources: Ammonium Phosphate, Ammonium Sulfate, Isobutylidene Diurea, Urea, Methylene Urea, Muriate of Potash.

Chlorine (Cl) not more than 10.0%
   *19.4% Slowly Available Nitrogen from Methylene Ureas and IBDU.

MAKING SENSE OF CYCLES

Using fertilizers with many synthetic ingredients has contributed to excessive amounts of nitrogen in the soil. Too much nitrogen can cause many problems with the environment. These problems include the build-up of nitrogen compounds that can cause high rates of acidity in the soil and actually reduce the growth of crops. Today, scientists have developed fertilizers that reduce the amount of synthetic fertilizer we put into the soil.

Shown here are labels from two bags of fertilizer. One contains many synthetic ingredients. The other contains more organic, or natural, ingredients. Look at each label and compare the lists of ingredients. Based on information you have gathered from reading this book, see if you can identify which label is for organic fertilizer and which is for synthetic, or human-made, fertilizer. What kinds of ingredients seem more organic to you and why?

Greenhouse Gases

Earth's atmosphere has always contained gases that keep the planet warm and able to support life. The most common of these is carbon dioxide (CO_2). Another one, nitrous oxide (N_2O), is also present in small amounts in our atmosphere.

In recent years, the amount of these gases in our atmosphere has increased dramatically. That's largely because humans are burning more and more fossil fuels.

As the concentration of all these gases increases, Earth's atmosphere starts to act like a greenhouse. Just like a garden greenhouse, the atmosphere traps more and more of the Sun's heat. And like a greenhouse, our atmosphere becomes warmer than it would naturally be. This is called **climate change**, and the gases are called greenhouse gases.

MAKING SENSE OF CYCLES

Over time, some soil becomes less and less able to support crops. Why do you think that some crops have difficulty growing in certain kinds of soil over the years, and what can be done to solve this problem? Use information and evidence discussed in this book to support your thinking.

This power plant burning fossil fuels in England pours a large quantity of greenhouse gases into the atmosphere. These gases, which include carbon dioxide and nitrous oxide, increase the effects of climate change on our planet.

Here are some things you can do to help the nitrogen cycle:

- Avoid using artificial fertilizers in your garden or make sure you don't use more fertilizer than your plants need. Read the directions on the package!
- Learn about crop rotation for your garden. Some plants put nitrogen into the soil, while others take it out. Rotating plantings between these two types of plants, or letting part of the soil lie fallow, or unused, for a period of time, will help balance the nitrogen cycle.
- *Never* burn trash in your backyard! That adds nitrogen oxides to the air, and those contribute to smog and air pollution.
- Steer clear of the drive-thru at restaurants and other businesses. Sitting in the car with the engine running pumps nitrogen oxides into the air. Park the car and go inside to place your order.
- Learn as much as you can about the nitrogen cycle. Someday you may be a scientist who helps get the cycle back in balance!

Warmer temperatures mean that glaciers and Arctic ice melt and ocean levels could rise. Higher temperatures may also cause excessive rainfall and flooding in some areas, and reduced rainfall and **droughts**, or dry spells, in others. Without enough rainfall, crops don't grow properly. Rising global temperatures also lead to unusual weather patterns and natural disasters. Hurricanes, wildfires, and lightning storms may not appear to be related to global warming and other forms of climate change, but they are.

Nitrous oxide accounts for just six percent of greenhouse gases. Nitrous oxide is 300 times as powerful as carbon dioxide when it comes to trapping warm air, however. So even that smaller amount can have a huge impact.

Rice plants struggle to grow through parched soil during a drought.

For years, humans have been using fossil fuels and synthetic fertilizers. These substances have increased levels of nitrogen compounds in Earth's air, soil, and water. These compounds have contributed to climate change, pollution, and acid rain. They can also choke off oxygen supplies to aquatic plants and animals.

Based on the information contained in this book, and on some of the other questions you've seen so far, think about what sources of excess nitrogen seem most obvious to you as ones to tackle first. Based on your thinking, what are three things you would suggest that scientists and engineers investigate as ways of reducing excess nitrogen and restoring balance to the nitrogen cycle?

Rebalancing the Cycle

For years, scientists and engineers have been working to find ways to reduce humans' use of fossil fuels. That will help reduce the production of nitrogen oxides, and therefore reduce acid rain and air pollution.

Some researchers are developing electric cars, airplanes that run on solar power, and trains that are pulled along their tracks by magnetic forces. Others are looking into new and renewable sources of fuel. Wind power and rising-and-falling tides are being explored as potential energy sources.

Australian inventor Buzz Burrows proudly displays a type of organic fertilizer made in his special toilet, called a Rota-Loo. The toilet uses bacteria and heat to control the rotting of human excrement, or waste. The end product is odorless, and doesn't rely on synthetic ingredients. Using a Rota-Loo, humans can produce several pounds of organic fertilizer every month. Now when someone asks, "How does your garden grow?" you can decide how best to tell them!

The bigger concern when it comes to the nitrogen cycle, though, is the use of synthetic fertilizers. For the past century, manufacturing and using these synthetic products have been the main cause of the rise of nitrous oxide and of upsetting the nitrogen cycle.

Scientists and engineers are looking for ways to change that.

Researchers have developed organic, natural, non-synthetic fertilizers. These people continue to work on ways to make fertilizers even more effective and less damaging. Others are looking at different ways of applying fertilizers to plants, such as using fewer harmful ingredients. Another goal is to figure out a way to help crops absorb more nitrogen, so less nitrogen washes into the soil. Engineers are exploring new ways of dealing with run-off from farm fields, to keep nitrogen-rich water out of streams and lakes.

N_2O = LAUGHING GAS

On Earth, man-made nitrous oxide (N_2O) is mostly used as an **anesthetic** or **sedative**. That means doctors and dentists use it to calm patients or put them to sleep during medical or dental procedures. If you inhale just a little bit—not enough to put you to sleep—nitrous oxide gives you a happy feeling. Because of that, it is known as "laughing gas."

Some scientists are working with plants to develop crops that produce more food. That would mean farmers could plant fewer crops and use less fertilizer to get the same quantities of fruit, vegetables, or grains.

Other scientists and engineers are studying the effects of nitrogen on air, soil, and water. The better they understand these effects, the more we all can do to rebalance the nitrogen cycle and keep our planet healthy.

Seedlings being planted in a dry area of the African nation of Senegal. The men are adding water containing nitrogen-fixing bacteria to the soil around the plant's roots. The bacteria will live in nodules on the plant's roots and convert nitrogen in the atmosphere to compounds the plants can use. Methods such as these will allow farming in dry places, reduce the need for fertilizers, and help keep nitrogen moving through its cycle.

Is Nitrogen Necessary?

Fertilizers contain nitrogen in the form of compounds such as nitrates and ammonia. Soil naturally contains these compounds, but eventually they get used up and need to be replaced.

So how important is nitrogen to plant growth?

In this activity, you will plant bean seeds in three paper cups of vermiculite. Vermiculite is a product used to start seeds, and it does not contain nitrogen. In the following days, you will water one paper cup with water only, one cup with water plus liquid fertilizer containing nitrogen, and one cup with water plus double-strength fertilizer. As you observe the growth of the plants, think about what you are seeing and draw conclusions about the importance of nitrogen to plant growth and health.

You Will Need

- 6 bean seeds
- Bottle of liquid plant fertilizer with label showing nitrogen content of at least 10%
- 3 8–9-ounce (250-mL) paper cups
- Pencil
- Newspaper
- Small bag of vermiculite, available at a garden center
- 3 bottles of drinking water
- Pan or tray to put under the cups
- Tablespoon
- Marking pen
- Notebook or pad of paper and pen or pencil

Instructions

1 Spread a sheet of newspaper on your work area.

2 Label the paper cups and the water bottles: #1, #2, and #3.

3 Poke a drainage hole in the bottom of each cup with a pencil.

Bottle 1 Bottle 2 Bottle 3

4 Fill each cup at least ¾ full of vermiculite.

5 Add tap water until the vermiculite is soaked. Allow to drain. Do not let vermiculite go down the drain.

6 Add four drops of liquid fertilizer to Bottle #1 and eight drops to Bottle #2. Shake gently to mix. Bottle #3 contains only water.

7 Plant two bean seeds in each cup. Put cups on tray and place in a sunny location.

8 Check on cups at least twice a day. As the vermiculite starts drying out, add a tablespoon of water from each bottle to its partner cup. The vermiculite should be kept damp but not soggy.

9 If you run out of water in the bottles, refill with tap water and add the same number of drops of fertilizer as you started with.

11 Observe the plant growth every day for about three weeks and take notes, recording what you observe.

10 Seeds should sprout in 3 to 10 days.

The Challenge

After three weeks, present your investigation to others, explaining what you did and what you have discovered. Think about and discuss:

- Any differences you've observed among the plants in the three cups.
- How these differences might be related to the strength of nitrogen-containing fertilizer that plants #1 and #2 were given.
- What might happen to plant #3 over time if it continues to receive only water and no nitrogen.
- How nitrogen as a plant nutrient is part of the larger nitrogen cycle.

GLOSSARY

acid rain Rainfall produced by certain chemicals in the atmosphere combined with rain to make it more acidic

amino acid Molecules made of nitrogen, carbon, oxygen, and hydrogen atoms that combine to make proteins in plants and animals

ammonia A molecule produced in the fixation and ammonification steps of the nitrogen cycle

ammonification A step in the nitrogen cycle in which the nitrogen in decaying plants and animals is converted to ammonia

anesthetic A chemical used by doctors and dentists to put patients to sleep during surgery

aquatic Of or relating to water

assimilation A step in the nitrogen cycle in which nitrogen is absorbed and used by plants

atmosphere The layer of gases surrounding Earth

atom The basic unit of a chemical element. Atoms make up all living and nonliving things

bacteria Single-celled organisms. Bacteria are responsible for many steps in the nitrogen cycle

beneficial Producing something good or helpful

blue-green algae A type of bacteria found in bodies of water. Also called cyanobacteria

chlorophyll A green chemical in plant leaves that absorbs energy from the Sun and begins the process of photosynthesis

climate change The gradual increase in the temperature of Earth's atmosphere due to the increased levels of greenhouse gases

compound Atoms and molecules that bond together to form a new substance

cyanobacteria A type of bacteria found in bodies of water. Also called blue-green algae

denitrification A step in the nitrogen cycle in which bacteria convert nitrogen or nitrogen compounds to nitrogen gas

drought A long period of dryness, with no rain. Usually results in damage to food crops

electron A tiny, negatively charged particle of energy in an atom

element A pure chemical substance. Each element contains only one type of atom

elimination Removal

enzyme A type of protein that drives different processes in a plant or animal

filament The wire inside a light bulb

fossil fuel A fuel source that began as organisms or plant material buried deep beneath Earth's surface underwent decomposition and other natural processes, usually over periods of millions of years, and were eventually converted to oil, coal, or natural gas

inert Of or referring to a chemical that does not react with others

legume A plant of the pea family, including beans, peas, lentils, and peanuts, containing seeds in pods and usually root nodules with nitrogen-fixing bacteria

microscopic So small as to be visible only with a microscope

molecule A particle formed when two or more atoms bond together

neutron A neutral particle found in the nucleus of an atom

nitrification A step in the nitrogen cycle in which bacteria convert ammonia or other nitrogen compounds to nitrates that plants can use

nitrogen fixation A step in the nitrogen cycle in which bacteria convert nitrogen gas to ammonia

nodule A swelling on a root of a plant, usually containing nitrogen-fixing bacteria

noxious Poisonous or harmful

nucleus The dense center of an atom containing protons and neutrons

Periodic Table of Elements A table that shows all known chemical elements, in order of atomic number, or the number of protons in the atom's nucleus

photosynthesis A process by which plants convert carbon dioxide, water, and sunlight into oxygen and sugars

protein Nitrogen compounds made of amino acids. Proteins are found in every living thing and are responsible for structure, chemical reactions, growth, and many other functions in the life of a plant or animal

proton A positively charged particle in the nucleus of an atom

sedative A drug taken for its calming or sleep-inducing effects

stable In a condition that is not likely to change

suffocate To smother. An animal that dies because of a lack of oxygen suffocates

symbiotic relationship A relationship between two organisms that benefits both organisms

BOOKS

Farndon, John. *Nitrogen* (The Elements). New York: Benchmark Books, 1999.

Hasan, Heather. *Nitrogen* (Understanding the Elements of the Periodic Table). New York: Rosen Publishing Group, 2005.

Slade, Suzanne. *The Nitrogen Cycle* (Cycles in Nature). New York: Rosen Publishing Group, 2007.

WEBSITES

www.pbslearningmedia.org/resource/nves.sci.earth.nitrate/lightning-produces-nitrates/
If you want to learn more about lightning's role in the nitrogen cycle, check out this five-minute video. It shows amazing footage from space, while presenting all the information you need to understand this process. The Public Broadcasting Service (PBS) produced this web page—and it's a good one!

www.statedclearly.com/what-is-dna/
The website, called *Stated Clearly: Science is for everyone!*, features five videos, with many more planned. This particular video is called "What is DNA and how does it work?" It is a clear, colorful, five-minute visual explanation about DNA, its structure, and function.

www.visionlearning.com/en/library/Earth-Science/6/The-Nitrogen-Cycle/98
The Vision Learning website offers well-organized, easy-to-read science lessons. "The Nitrogen Cycle" page is typical of the website. It is divided into sections, each with its own summary, glossary, and quiz to test your knowledge.

news.nationalgeographic.com/news/2013/04/pictures/130423-extreme-algae-bloom-fertilizer-lake-erie-science/
National Geographic is known for its brilliant photographs. This web page shows amazing but disturbing pictures of out-of-control algae blooms around the world.

ABOUT THE AUTHOR

Diane Dakers was born and raised in Toronto, and now makes her home in Victoria, British Columbia, Canada. She has been a newspaper, television, and radio journalist since 1991. Learning about the nitrogen cycle has helped her grow a healthier garden!